Written by Marjorie Redford
Illustrated by Kathryn Marlin

Published by Standard Publishing, Cincinnati, Ohio

www.standardpub.com

ISBN 978-0-7847-2293-0

17 16 15 14 13 12   5 6 7 8 9 10 11 12 13

Cincinnati, Ohio

My Bible says God made the world and everything that's in it.

"In the beginning, God created the sky and the earth. . . . and it was very good." *Genesis 1:1, 31*

My Bible says God made me—
from head to toe he did it!

"I praise you because you made me in an amazing and wonderful way." *Psalm 139:14*

My Bible says that God is great.
He helps me every day.

"Our Lord is great and very powerful." *Psalm 147:5*

"Our help comes from the Lord, who made heaven and earth." *Psalm 124:8*

My Bible says to love the Lord. I can serve him on my way.

"Love the Lord your God with all your heart, soul and strength." *Deuteronomy 6:5*

"Serve the Lord with all your heart." *1 Samuel 12:20*

My Bible says that God is good.
His love will never end.

"Thank the Lord because he is good.
His love continues forever." *Psalm 107:1*

My Bible says God sent his Son.
Jesus is my best friend!

"Jesus is the Christ,
the Son of God." *John 20:31*

My Bible says to love each other,
no matter what we do.

"A friend loves you all the time." *Proverbs 17:17*

"We should love each other, because love comes from God." *1 John 4:7*

My Bible says to go tell others, "Jesus loves you too!"

"Go everywhere in the world. Tell the Good News to everyone." *Mark 16:15*